HOW THE FUTURE BEGAN:

COMMUNICATIONS

HOW THE FUTURE BEGAN:

BEGAN:

COMMUNICATIONS

ANTHONY WILSON

KING*f*ISHER

NEW YORK

Author
Anthony Wilson

Senior Editor
Clive Wilson

Senior Designer
Mike Buckley

DTP Coordinator
Nicky Studdart

Production Controller
Caroline Jackson

Picture Research Manager
Jane Lambert

Indexer
Hilary Bird

KINGFISHER
Larousse Kingfisher Chambers Inc.
95 Madison Avenue
New York, New York 10016

First published in 1999
1 3 5 7 9 10 8 6 4 2

1TR / 0299 / TWP / RNB(RNB) / 135NMA

LIBRARY OF CONGRESS CATALOGING–IN–PUBLICATION DATA
Wilson, Anthony
How the future began. Communication / Anthony Wilson.—1st ed.
p. cm.
Includes index.
Summary: Surveys the field of communication, with an emphasis on
modern developments in telecommunication and the use of computers.
1. Telecommunication—Juvenile literature. 2. Computers—Juvenile
literature. [1. Telecommunication. 2. Communication.
3. Computers.] I. Title: Communication.
TK5102.4.W55 1999 621. 382–dc21 98-39795 CIP AC

ISBN 0-7534-5179-4
Printed in Singapore

CONTENTS

INTRODUCTION

We are living at a special moment in the world's history—not just the start of a new millennium, but the beginning of a new technological era. The past two hundred years have been the Industrial Age, based on machines, motors, and energy. Now we are moving into the Information Age, driven by microprocessors—the "brains" inside computers, cellular phones, and many other electronic devices.

The chapters in this book show how human lives in the Information Age will be different from lives today and in the past. New inventions will bring fresh possibilities, affecting where we live, the way we learn, the work we do, and how we choose to spend our leisure time.

To understand the future, we should also look into the past, because that is where the future began. Discoveries made by scientists two centuries ago led to new and faster ways of communicating, such as the electric telegraph and the telephone. Movies, radio, and television followed, but the turning point came with the invention of transistors and lasers in the mid-20th century. Without them, computers, the Internet, and all the high-speed communication systems of today and tomorrow could not exist.

No one can say exactly what the future will be like. Some of the events predicted in this book may never happen, and others will come sooner or later than predicted. There will also be totally unexpected developments, bringing possibilities that no one has yet dreamed of. But one prediction is certain—whatever our electronic future has in store, it will be an exciting time to be alive.

2200?
Human brain, connected to microchips, able to survive outside body

2060?
Intelligent computers built using "neural net" technology

2050?
Many factories totally automated

2050?
Microchips with ten trillion transistors become available

2025?
Computers speak, listen, and have other senses

2020?
"Flexiviewer" computer developed to fit in pocket

2020?
Cars drive themselves on main roads

2010?
First billion-transistor chip

1977
Personal computers (PCs) sold in stores

"When five computers have been sold, the world won't need any more," predicted the head of the computer firm IBM in the 1940s. Since then, computers have developed from simple number crunchers to powerful multipurpose information and communication machines that have revolutionized the way we live—and in the late 1990s, computers were selling at the rate of five every second. In the last fifty years, they have also increased in power an astonishing ten billion times. In the next half century, computers will continue to develop at a phenomenal rate, doubling in power every eighteen months. When they have their own sense systems and the ability to learn, they will begin to reason more like humans, becoming self-aware and learning from their mistakes. Computers will be everywhere, working away, often invisibly, inside every machine and gadget. By 2020, in the world's more developed countries, it is estimated that there could be as many as a hundred times more computers than people.

LIVING WITH COMPUTERS

1971
Pocket calculators go on sale

1970
First microprocessor made

1958
First integrated circuit

1947
Transistor invented

1940s
First electronic computers built in Britain and the U.S.

1834
Babbage plans a mechanical computer

AGE OF THE MICROPROCESSOR

In the time it takes to say "microprocessor," half a billion new transistors are made in factories around the world. Transistors are tiny electric switches, some so small that you need a microscope to see them. Huge numbers of them can be linked together to make complex circuits called microprocessors.

Microprocessors, also called microchips, are probably the most important invention of the last five centuries. Computers, televisions, telephones, and other electrical equipment in homes, cars, offices, and factories all rely on microchips to function— without them our lives would be very different. And without microchips none of the changes predicted in this book could ever happen.

△ Early transistors were small enough to make portable radios a reality in the early 1950s. By the 1970s, most transistors were built into microchips.

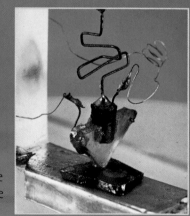

▷ The first transistor was constructed in the U.S. in 1947. Made partly from the material germanium, this primitive device went on to change the modern world.

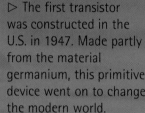

△ During the 1960s, computers like the IBM 702 filled a large room. They were prone to frequent breakdowns and had much less computing power than today's home computers.

▷ Microchips flooded onto the market during the 1970s, after new techniques made it possible to manufacture ready-wired circuits, containing tiny transistors and other components, in a single process.

"The day the future began"

On December 23, 1947, three American scientists demonstrated the world's first transistor, built from a paperclip, gold foil, and a slab of shiny material called germanium. Fifty years later, transistors outnumbered humans by a million to one. In fact, there could be at least ten million of these tiny switches in your home at this moment. Before transistors were available, radios, televisions, and computers used much larger electric valves. If one of today's digital phones used valves in place of transistors, it would be as big as a skyscraper.

▽ A typical computer contains a microprocessor and a number of other silicon chips. Each chip does a particular job and contains thousands of switching devices, or transistors. Wires called 'feet' connect the chips to the computer.

Miniaturization

As transistors become smaller, microprocessors become more powerful. By 2010, transistors will be so small that 2,000 of them will fit across the width of a single human hair. Billion-transistor microchips will be common, and computers will come on a single microchip. According to the man who invented the microprocessor, Federico Faggin, microchips containing ten thousand billion transistors will be available by 2050.

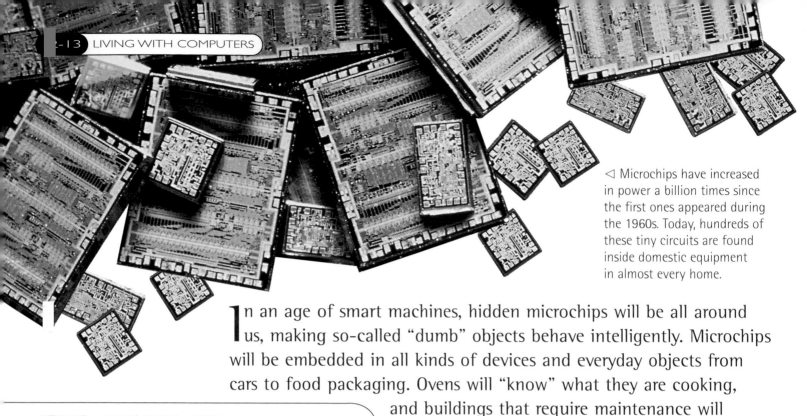

◁ Microchips have increased in power a billion times since the first ones appeared during the 1960s. Today, hundreds of these tiny circuits are found inside domestic equipment in almost every home.

In an age of smart machines, hidden microchips will be all around us, making so-called "dumb" objects behave intelligently. Microchips will be embedded in all kinds of devices and everyday objects from cars to food packaging. Ovens will "know" what they are cooking, and buildings that require maintenance will

CHIPS WITH EVERYTHING

alert engineers automatically. Smart cards—like credit cards but with a microchip inside—will be commonplace, communicating by radio with the external world. Personally coded so that no one else can use them, smart cards will open locked doors, carry data such as medical records, and, of course, be used instead of cash.

△▷ Although inefficient and difficult to operate, this vacuum cleaner from 1910 was an exciting novelty. Its microchip-controlled successor in the 21st century will no longer require human help to keep the house clean.

Sensing the world

Sensors are the key to the intelligent future. These miniature devices will come in many different forms and connect computers and other machines to the outside world. Using tiny microphones, machines will recognize voices and sounds. Mini video cameras and radar will enable machines to "see" their surroundings and navigate around obstacles, while infrared sensors will monitor human movement by body heat.

▽ Microchip-powered controls and indicators inside a cockpit enable pilots to land an aircraft safely in the dark.

▷ Intelligent buildings, such as this Japanese museum, can adapt to changing conditions, automatically switching from solar energy to conventional sources when necessary.

At home

Kitchen equipment first showed signs of becoming "smart" as long ago as the 1930s, when ovens were first equipped with thermostats and a little later with automatic timers. However, many of these devices were often complicated to use and they frequently malfunctioned. Advances in microchip technology will continue to make most household machines and gadgets much more efficient and user-friendly.

Saving the planet

Smarter homes mean a cleaner, greener environment. Improved microchip controls for lighting and heating will save energy, while a proposed intelligent garbage can will crush garbage, remove its smell, and sort it into different materials for recycling. All new cars will be fitted with automatic controls that fine tune the engine to reduce pollution and ensure that every drop of energy is extracted from the fuel.

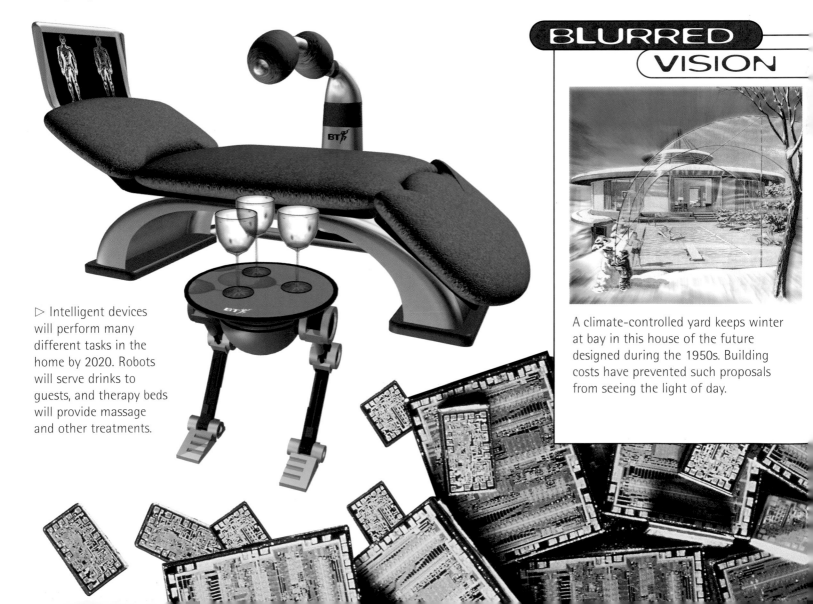

BLURRED VISION

A climate-controlled yard keeps winter at bay in this house of the future designed during the 1950s. Building costs have prevented such proposals from seeing the light of day.

▷ Intelligent devices will perform many different tasks in the home by 2020. Robots will serve drinks to guests, and therapy beds will provide massage and other treatments.

COMPUTERS IN CONTROL

△ Robby the Robot caught the public imagination in the 1956 movie *Forbidden Planet*. Karel Čapek adopted the term "robot" in 1920. It comes from a Czech word meaning "forced labor."

When a new computer-controlled luggage handling system was tested at Denver International Airport in 1994, chaos ensued. Automatic carts crashed into walls, and bags were taken to all the wrong places. The problem was traced to a bug—a human error in the instructions given to the computer. This incident demonstrated that intelligent machines still have serious limitations.

The breakthrough will come by 2010, when computer-controlled machines will be intelligent enough to learn from their own mistakes and find a way around any bugs in their software. Smart machines will be found not just in airports, but also in hospitals, shopping malls, factories, garages, and in our homes.

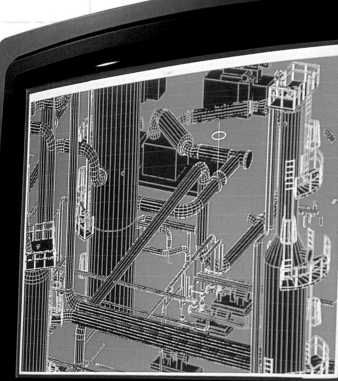

△ Concept cars such as this one may go into production by the year 2005. Computer design ensures perfect streamlining and maximum fuel efficiency.

Danger zones

In 1979, the robot Rover 1 helped prevent a major catastrophe when it was sent in to repair the damaged nuclear reactor at Three Mile Island. As computer power increases, robots will take over more and more tasks from humans in dangerous places—whether it is in a nuclear reactor, on the ocean floor, or in a raging forest fire. With laser-guided bombs and pilotless fighter planes, some future wars will be fought between advanced computer systems—watched over by human controllers far from the battle zone.

Self-sufficiency

In the 1990s, the first fully-automated factories gave a glimpse of what lies ahead. Working 24 hours a day, machines performed complex tasks, such as testing chemicals for drug manufacture or assembling TV sets and cellular phones. Humans were nowhere to be seen, apart from one or two highly skilled engineers needed to oversee the computers and machines in case anything went wrong. By 2050, the majority of factories will be like this.

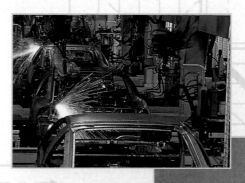

◁ Robot welders became a familiar sight in car factories in the 1980s. Robots perform best when doing repetitive jobs.

▷ During the 1991 Gulf War, automated bombs homed in with pinpoint accuracy on targets picked out by laser beams.

◁ Architects and designers rely on computers to help them visualize complex three-dimensional structures, such as these factories. Future computers will play an even more important role in building and testing, as well as design.

Beyond our planet

Robot craft have already traveled much farther into space than humans. Early space explorers included the two Viking landers, sent to Mars in the 1970s. In 1997, the robot rover Sojourner spent three months analyzing rocks on Mars. By 2010, it is expected that robot explorers will bring back dust from a comet and visit Pluto, the outermost planet in the solar system.

CRYSTAL BALL

As robots become more intelligent and versatile, they will reach the point where they begin to design and build improved versions of themselves. Some futurists predict that by 2100, robots may have even become the most intelligent form of life on Earth.

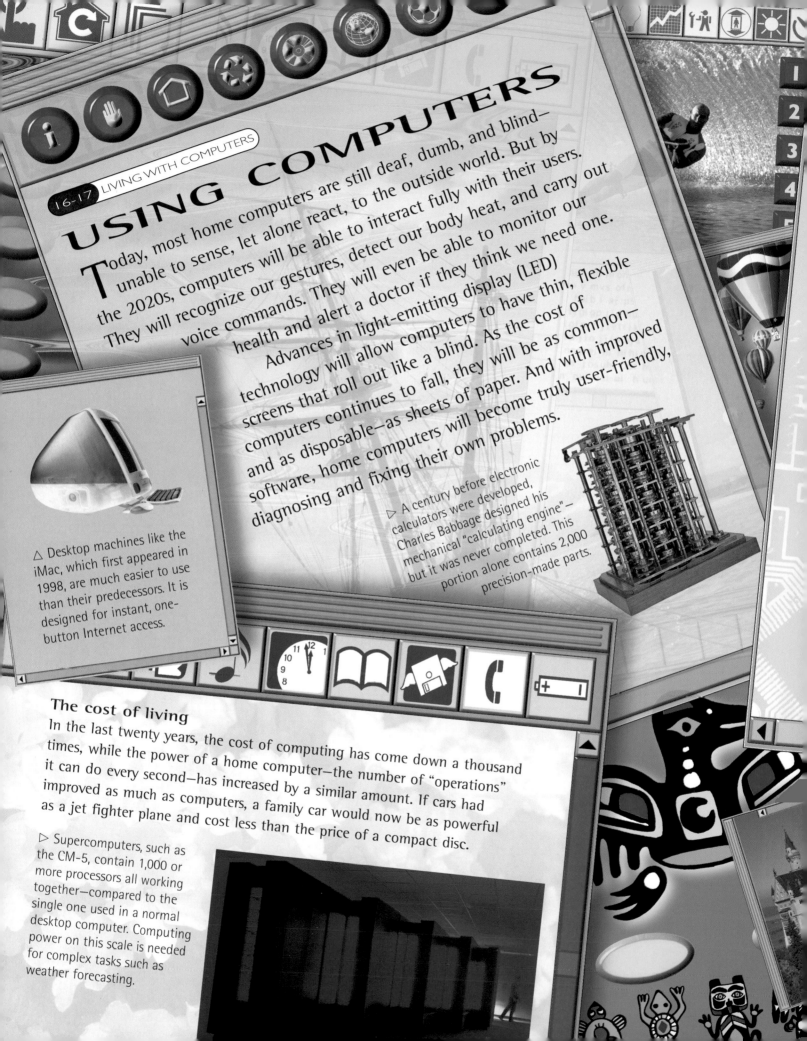

USING COMPUTERS

Today, most home computers are still deaf, dumb, and blind—unable to sense, let alone react, to the outside world. But by the 2020s, computers will be able to interact fully with their users. They will recognize our gestures, detect our body heat, and carry out voice commands. They will even be able to monitor our health and alert a doctor if they think we need one.

Advances in light-emitting display (LED) technology will allow computers to have thin, flexible screens that roll out like a blind. As the cost of computers continues to fall, they will be as common—and as disposable—as sheets of paper. And with improved software, home computers will become truly user-friendly, diagnosing and fixing their own problems.

△ Desktop machines like the iMac, which first appeared in 1998, are much easier to use than their predecessors. It is designed for instant, one-button Internet access.

▷ A century before electronic calculators were developed, Charles Babbage designed his mechanical "calculating engine"—but it was never completed. This portion alone contains 2,000 precision-made parts.

The cost of living

In the last twenty years, the cost of computing has come down a thousand times, while the power of a home computer—the number of "operations" it can do every second—has increased by a similar amount. If cars had improved as much as computers, a family car would now be as powerful as a jet fighter plane and cost less than the price of a compact disc.

▷ Supercomputers, such as the CM-5, contain 1,000 or more processors all working together—compared to the single one used in a normal desktop computer. Computing power on this scale is needed for complex tasks such as weather forecasting.

◁ A large color display will be the main feature of this "flexiviewer" personal communicator predicted for the year 2020. The magazine-sized screen scrolls down to fit in a pocket when not in use.

One box for all

Forty years ago, the first commercial computers were slow number crunchers, mostly good for solving numerical problems. With no keyboard or screen, they were far harder to communicate with than today's more powerful computers. However, with videophone, television, and the Internet built into one portable unit, personal computers will become even more versatile, as well as smaller and faster than current machines.

◁ By 2005, lightweight, portable computers will be voice-controlled and recognize handwriting. A solar-powered microphone and earpiece (*below*) will be linked to the main unit by radio.

△ By 2050, home computers may resemble sheets of paper —thin, flexible screens with a microchip inside. They will come in tear-off pads and will be widely available. A radio link will connect them to a central processor and to the Internet.

Light beams and particles

By 2010, high-powered computers will work so quickly—a million billion calculations a second—that wire connections will be useless. Only light rays will move fast enough to carry data inside these "optical" machines. By 2050, quantum computers will use and manipulate subatomic particles. These will solve in seconds problems that can take years of work by today's supercomputers.

▷ Cybercafés, where machines are available for rent, provide low-cost Internet access and the chance to communicate with people from around the world.

HANDLING INFORMATION

Before we reach the year 2010, it will be possible to pack all of the information in a library of 2,000 books onto a single microchip no larger than your thumbnail. Retrieving data from this billion-byte memory chip will take only a few millionths of a second. Today's limited and sluggish computer storage systems, such as magnetic discs and CD-ROMs, will be a distant memory. Information can be stored on the Internet, too. To help us navigate through the vast and ever-expanding sea of data, we will depend on "intelligent agents." These digital assistants will learn our needs and automatically search the Internet, for relevant information.

▷ For nearly 2,000 years, books have been vital for storing and providing information. Before printing was invented, handwritten books were rare and treasured possessions.

Photographic memory
Fifty years ago, the first computers had tiny memories that stored no more than a thousand bytes. Today, a home computer stores millions times more than this in its internal memory chips and hard disk. Silicon chips might be suceeded by holographic memories. These will pack hundreds of billions of bytes into tiny patterns in layers of photographic film. By 2020, a single holographic memory unit will be able to hold as much data as all the world's computers did in 1998.

△ The greater part of human knowledge is stored in libraries around the world. People have kept written records in one form or another for over 5,500 years.

CRYSTAL BALL

By 2200, the human brain may be kept alive without any body at all, connected instead to microchips, artificial senses, and other support systems. Such a being might live forever—or until someone else decided to switch it off.

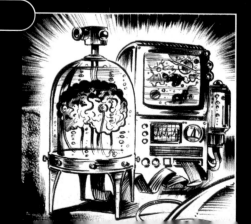

Brain power

Today's computers store information in electronic boxes—to retrieve the data you simply open the right box. But pioneers are developing new memory systems that work like the human brain, where memories are stored by association, each memory connected to many similar ones. Ultimately, these memory chips may be linked directly to our brains.

△ Writing was the earliest way of preserving knowledge other than in our heads. These Ancient Egyptian hieroglyphs, or picture signs, were carved in stone just over 3,000 years ago.

▷ In the 1990s, CD-ROMs became a very important storage system. A single disc can store the equivalent of 60 million words.

The book

One essential way to store and share ideas and information has remained popular for more than 500 years. It is the technology in front of you now—a printed book. In the future, many books and magazines will be downloaded from the Internet, but printed matter is unlikely to be completely replaced.

▷ Intelligent agents called "knowbots" will not only filter specific information from the Internet but also assess whether it comes from a reliable source. A human face makes the agent more user-friendly.

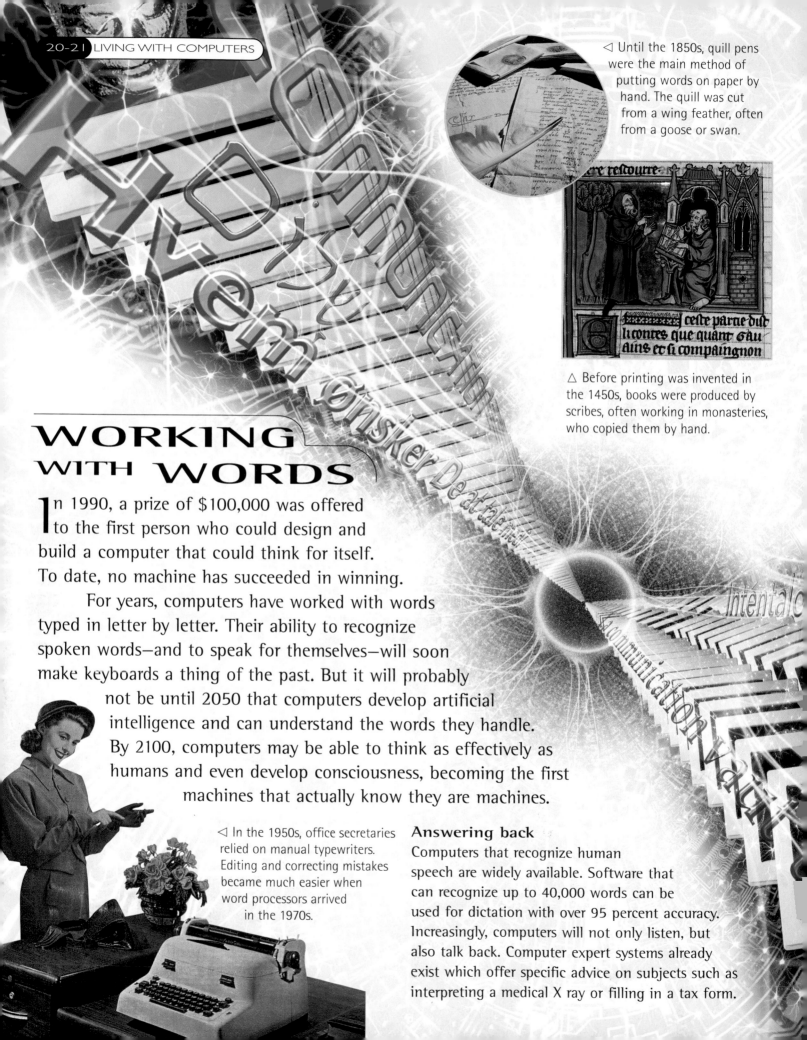

◁ Until the 1850s, quill pens were the main method of putting words on paper by hand. The quill was cut from a wing feather, often from a goose or swan.

△ Before printing was invented in the 1450s, books were produced by scribes, often working in monasteries, who copied them by hand.

WORKING WITH WORDS

In 1990, a prize of $100,000 was offered to the first person who could design and build a computer that could think for itself. To date, no machine has succeeded in winning.

For years, computers have worked with words typed in letter by letter. Their ability to recognize spoken words—and to speak for themselves—will soon make keyboards a thing of the past. But it will probably not be until 2050 that computers develop artificial intelligence and can understand the words they handle. By 2100, computers may be able to think as effectively as humans and even develop consciousness, becoming the first machines that actually know they are machines.

◁ In the 1950s, office secretaries relied on manual typewriters. Editing and correcting mistakes became much easier when word processors arrived in the 1970s.

Answering back

Computers that recognize human speech are widely available. Software that can recognize up to 40,000 words can be used for dictation with over 95 percent accuracy. Increasingly, computers will not only listen, but also talk back. Computer expert systems already exist which offer specific advice on subjects such as interpreting a medical X ray or filling in a tax form.

Improving efficiency

In the late 20th century, millions of jobs disappeared as powerful computers were used to handle words and figures automatically, working much faster than humans can. For people who still have jobs, computers that talk and listen will help them work much more efficiently. In 2020, it has been estimated that people in some jobs will achieve as much in a month as their parents could in a whole year.

Human role model

Today, most computers can only do one thing at a time, but they do it extremely fast. Human brains are much slower, but can do many things at once, using a network of billions of neuron nerve cells. Some experts believe that computers will only begin to become really intelligent some time after 2050, when they, too, are made of neural nets—the electronic version of our own brain cells.

◁ Calligraphy—the art of beautiful writing—is still highly valued in China. Chinese characters and the techniques for drawing them have changed little in the past 4,000 years.

▷ The human brain contains a network of at least ten billion special cells called neurons. By 2050, computers may rely on networks of electronic neurons.

▽ A new generation of "neural net" computers that mimic the way the human brain works would finally enable machines to translate text and spoken words from one language to another as effectively as humans.

1965
First communications satellite relays 240 phone calls at once

1956
First telephone cable under the Atlantic

1930s
All five continents linked by radiotelephone

1901
Marconi sends first radio messages across the Atlantic

1876
Bell invents the telephone

1837
First public demonstration of telegraph

2015?
Holophone projects lifelike 3-D images

2010?
Most homes have fiber-optic link to the outside world

2008?
Personal communicator combines computer, videophone, and Internet access in one portable unit

2005?
Children allocated a personal number they keep for life

KEEPING IN TOUCH

1974
Arpanet, the forerunner of the Internet, links 62 computers

ARPANET

1976
First e-mails sent

1983
First cellular phone service

1991
Start of World Wide Web

1992
One million sites linked by the Internet

2002?
Cellular videophones become popular

2005?
Hundreds of new satellites and make cellular phones and the Internet available worldwide

Two centuries ago, even the most urgent message traveled no faster than a horse could gallop. In the 1840s, electricity began to dramatically change the way we communicate. Copper wires crisscrossed towns, countries, and continents, carrying first the letter-by-letter coded words of the electric telegraph and, later, actual speech by telephone.

By the 1990s, copper wire was making way for glass fibers that can carry several million times more information. Rivaling this ground-based system is the invisible network of wireless communication that uses radio waves to transmit words and data at the speed of light.

Early in the 21st century, telephone and Internet will merge, providing person-to-person communication that is cheaper, more convenient, and—using a 3-D process called holography—more lifelike. New satellite networks will make personal communication accessible to most of the world's population, half of whom have never used a telephone. It will be possible to reach another person anywhere on the planet.

IT'S GOOD TO TALK

It has been estimated that people born in the year 2000 will spend more than two years on the telephone during their lifetimes. Yet when the first telephones came into use during the 1870s, many people doubted whether the invention would catch on.

The telephone will continue to change our lives as the new century progresses. By 2010, cellular phones will work in most places on the planet, while automatic switching between fiber-optic and radio networks will provide high quality and inexpensive links to the global network. Children will get their own phone number as soon as they can speak, and keep the same number all their lives.

Making history

In 1876, the invention of the telephone by Alexander Graham Bell, a Scotsman who settled in the United States, marked the beginning of modern telecommunications. The first words picked up by his assistant in another room were "Mr. Watson, come here. I want you." In October that year, they held the first long-distance telephone conversation between Boston and Cambridge, Massachusetts—a distance of nearly two miles. By 1880, there were more than 70,000 subscribers to the new telephone service.

△ Until the invention of the telephone, the telegraph was the only way of sending long-distance messages rapidly.

▽ Alexander Graham Bell's 1876 telephone used separate devices for receiver and mouthpiece. At first, the general public showed little interest in his invention.

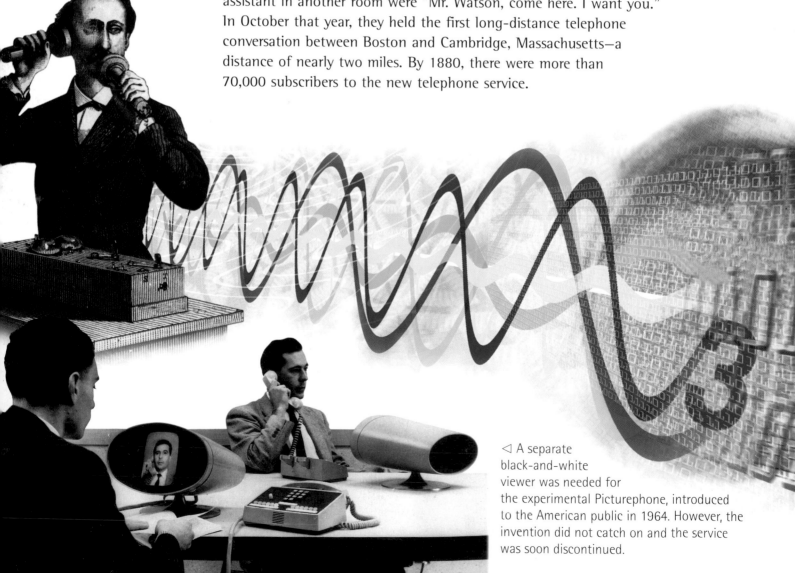

◁ A separate black-and-white viewer was needed for the experimental Picturephone, introduced to the American public in 1964. However, the invention did not catch on and the service was soon discontinued.

◁▽ Upright telephones gave way to the more familiar cradle version in the 1930s. Another innovation, the dial, brought a faster service for callers.

△ As well as conventional telephone calls, the dataphone, planned for 2005, allows images, text, and other visual data to be viewed on a small detachable eyepiece.

Full circle

The first messages sent by telegraph down electric wires used an early version of digital technology—each letter of the alphabet was coded into a pattern of short and long beeps. For many years after this, the telephone used an analog system where sound vibrations are converted into electrical vibrations and then back again. Today, we are heading for an all-digital future, when telephone messages (and radio and television broadcasts) are converted into a series of digits (zeros and ones). Digital transmission means that more data can be sent down a single cable and does not become distorted.

Innovations

The shift to all-digital technology is driving advances in communication devices. Cellular phones, for example, are becoming smaller and more cost-effective, while by 2005, videophones will transmit and receive high-quality images as well as high-fidelity sound.

▽ The changeover from analog to digital transmission, in which speech is coded into pulses made up of zeros and ones, will continue to bring better sound quality, cheaper calls, and new services for telephone users.

LINKED BY LASER

During the 1980s, an invisible revolution took place in the way we communicate. Laser light, passing down long, thin strands of glass called optical fibers, began to replace electricity and copper wires as the best way to carry telephone messages. By 1988, a single fiber-optic cable under the Atlantic Ocean was carrying 40,000 telephone conversations at the same time. By 2020, most homes in affluent countries will be joined to the communications network by two-way fiber-optic links, carrying high-quality sound and video for phones, multichannel television and radio, and other information services.

△ Early steamships were used to lay telegraph cables across the ocean floor. By 1874, all five continents were linked.

Crystal clear

Overhead phone wires, looping from poles to houses, have been part of the scenery for more than a century. Now they are disappearing fast, replaced by underground cables that carry glass fibers as thin as an eyelash. The glass is so clear that, in theory, it would be possible to see through a window made from it that was over 60 miles thick.

▽▷ Optical fibers, carrying thousands of phone calls down a single glass strand, have largely replaced overhead cables, which needed one wire for every phone call made.

◁ The first laser was made by American physicist Theodore Maiman in 1960. Laser stands for light amplification by stimulated emission of radiation. Laser light travels in an intense, narrow beam.

Pulses of light

The laser is a vital 20th century invention that will drive the communications network of the 21st century. Lasers used in communications supply a narrow beam of ultrapure infrared light. This can be emitted through fiber optics as a stream of tiny flashes. Because the laser can flash so fast—up to a thousand billion times a second—its beam can carry vast amounts of information. In fact, you could download all the pictures and words in a thousand books like this one in less than a second.

▷ Today, lasers are used not just in communications, but as laboratory tools, in CD players, bar-code readers, microsurgery, and in industry. The most powerful lasers can cut through metal and other materials.

△ The transmission of people through space, or teleportation, will still be impossible by 2015, but the holographic telephone will be the next best thing. Holophones will use lasers to re-create in real time a realistic 3-D image of the person at the other end of the line.

Avoiding bottlenecks
Traditional copper cable is known as a "narrowband" channel. It can only carry a limited amount of information. Fiber optics is "broadband"—it can transmit up to one hundred times the amount of information. However, to cope with the increasing speed and amount of data, the electronic switches at the receiving end will also have to be replaced by switches that are made from lasers.

▷ Individual strands of pure glass, many miles in length but much thinner than a human hair, are the backbone of modern communications. Coded pulses of laser light travel along each strand.

LOOK, NO WIRES!

▽ At just over 1,840 feet, Toronto's CN Tower is the tallest freestanding structure in the world and a vital link in Canada's radio communications network.

In 1912, one feeble radio message saved hundreds of lives. It was sent by the radio operator of the doomed ocean liner *Titanic* and was picked up by another ship close enough to rescue 700 passengers. Today, a similar type of "wire-less" communication is used by anyone who has a cellular phone. Radio waves, traveling through the air at the speed of light, relay messages between the phone and the nearest receiving tower or passing satellite.

By 2010, radio communication will be common inside homes and offices, too. The familiar tangle of cables that connect computers, printers, and other devices will disappear as more and more equipment becomes cordless, and data is sent and received instead by short-range radio links.

△ Wireless telegraphy, or radio, was first developed by the Italian scientist Guglielmo Marconi. He transmitted a message across his father's estate, and used a flat metal plate as his receiving antenna.

Wireless world

Until the 1890s, long-distance communication—either by telegraph or by telephone—was restricted to places that were connected by electric wires. Then, in 1895, Guglielmo Marconi succeeded in sending telegraph code signals through the air over a distance of about one mile. He soon discovered that the higher the receiving antenna, the greater the signals' range. In 1901, Marconi sent a radio message from Europe to America, and soon, millions of radio messages were flashing around the world every day.

BLURRED VISION

The personal radio receiver was predicted in 1909, half a century before transistors made miniature radios a reality. A frock coat and top hat were essential pieces of the equipment, carrying antenna and power supply respectively.

Phoning home

The phone service reached the
Moon in 1969, when President Richard
Nixon spoke to astronauts Neil Armstrong
and Edwin "Buzz" Aldrin on the lunar surface.
Speaking by radiotelephone, the president called
it "the most historic telephone call ever made."
Future space explorers will travel much farther
than the Moon but never be out of
touch with the Earth.

The world in your hand

Today's communications satellites are
fixed in orbits 22,500 miles above the
Earth's equator, relaying telephone calls and
other data between widely-separated receiving stations.
By 2010, a new generation of satellites will circle the
Earth in much lower orbits, crossing the sky from
horizon to horizon in just a few minutes. There will be
so many satellites that, wherever you are on the Earth,
there will always be one within range to handle your
cellular phone calls or connect you to the Internet.

△ A new generation of low-
orbit satellites is beginning
to handle cellular phone calls
worldwide. When complete,
the "Iridium" network will
include 66 solar-powered
satellites, orbiting 488
miles above the Earth.

▷ Videophones (*far right*) will be able to send and receive
images as well as speech and data by the year 2005.
The wristwatch version (*near right and center*), allowing
real time face-to-face video communication, will follow
a decade later.

Less an information superhighway than a bad case of gridlock has been many people's experience of the Internet during the 1990s. But by 2010, the early years of the Internet will be long forgotten. Broadband fiber-optic connections will bring a new high-speed Internet directly into homes and offices, with access so rapid that tasks like downloading an entire movie will take only a second or two. Fleets of new satellites will make this superNet accessible anywhere on Earth.

CAUGHT IN THE NET

Using miniature portable communicators, more than a billion enthusiasts around the world will rely on the Internet for information and entertainment as well as for business and personal communication.

◁ Tim Berners-Lee, a British mathematician, invented the system of linking one site to another that has made the World Wide Web so popular.

Going global

Computers worked in isolation from one another until 1961 when engineers in California succeeded in establishing a communications link between two machines. Soon, a telephone-based network of computers was developed in great secrecy. This network would function as an effective means of communication, even in the event of nuclear war. By the early 1990s, this system, known as Arpanet, had mushroomed into a vast global network of a million computers and was renamed the Internet.

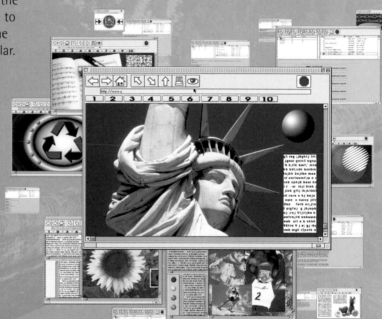

△ At first, websites—the "home pages" of organizations and people who use the Internet—only carried words, but pictures soon followed. In the future, broadband Internet will add high-quality sound, video, and many other features.

◁ During the 1960s, military officials at the Pentagon in Washington planned a new communication system that would allow scientists to contact each other after a nuclear war. The Internet eventually emerged out of this system.

Sending packets
One of the keys to the Internet's success is packet switching. Data is broken up into sections, each of which makes its own way through the Internet to the destination. There, another computer reassembles the original message. Packet switching makes the best use of the Internet's capacity and bypasses parts of the Internet that may be overloaded or out of action.

Spreading its net
The Internet will evolve in many different ways. It is already replacing more conventional ways of communicating, such as writing letters, publishing books and magazines, or simply pinning up notices on a bulletin board. Many experts believe the Internet will soon carry the world's telephone calls and much of its television and radio broadcasting, too.

△ A dense network of fiber optics provides the backbone of the Internet. Early in the 21st century, satellites will also bring Internet by radio to people on the move, and to parts of the globe that fiber optics cannot reach.

◁ The Internet's vital linking stations operate night and day. This one is in the high-security Telehouse building in London, England.

2010?
Miniature memory cards store music

2005?
Satellites bring high-quality radio broadcasting to developing countries

1998
Digital broadcasting introduced

1997
Deep Blue beats Gary Kasparov, world chess champion

1982
CDs begin replacing phonograph records

1975
VCRs become widely available

ENTERTAINMENT

Since the 1980s, millions of computers around the world have been designed and sold for one thing only—playing games. Videogame computers are only the latest in a long line of inventions that have included photography and movies, radio and television, the phonograph, personal stereos, CD players, and VCRs. All of these devices have one thing in common—they are designed to keep people entertained in their spare time.

In the early years of the 21st century, low-cost digital equipment will allow ordinary people to produce sounds and images that once required specialized equipment that had to be operated by experts. Digital technology will revolutionize broadcasting. There will be thousands of television channels to choose from—plus countless new Internet television and radio stations. If that is not enough, then the next generation of high-quality virtual reality systems should keep you occupied and entertained!

1962 Telstar satellite relays first television pictures between Europe and the U.S.

1949 Over a million people own television sets in the U.S.

1922 More than 500 radio stations operating in the U.S.

1920 Millions of people have phonographs

1895 Lumière brothers show first motion picture

1888 Kodak camera invented

VIRTUAL WORLDS

Since prehistoric times, humans have sometimes wanted to escape everyday reality and to transport themselves to new worlds. Today, using virtual reality technology, you can instantly immerse yourself in a computer-generated environment. Special headsets and data gloves give the impression of being inside an imaginary place in which you can move, float, or even fly.

By 2015, bodysuits packed with sensors and feedback devices will be widely available. With computers controlling the input to all the senses—taste and smell, as well as sight, sound, touch, and movement—users will experience entirely believable virtual worlds, from taking part in a historical battle to visiting another planet.

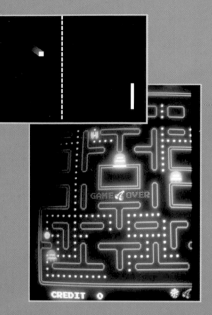

△ Commercial computer games first appeared in the 1970s. Although the graphics were crude, they were the introduction to computers for many people.

Beyond fun and games

Games and entertainment are major driving forces in the development of virtual reality technology. But it also has serious uses, such as the practice of delicate operations by surgeons or the training of fighter pilots. Scientists are also taking advantage of virtual reality. By manipulating virtual molecules, for example, they can begin to create new materials or learn about highly complex structures.

△ Coin-operated pinball machines were popular in arcades from the 1950s, until computerized arcade games began to replace them thirty years later.

Creating life

For many years, scientists have explored the way living things change and evolve by "breeding" digital life-forms in computers. Like real organisms, these electronic versions live, reproduce, and eventually die. As software develops, more intelligent forms of so-called Artificial Life will appear, spreading worldwide through the Internet. In the 21st century, advances in Artificial Life will lead to a new generation of computers that can learn, evolve, and even repair themselves.

△ A huge range of increasingly sophisticated games is available to players. Since the 1970s, computer games have developed into a hugely profitable and competitive industry with a global market.

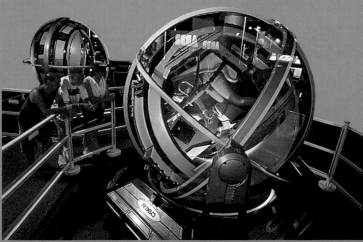

△ Advanced mechanical sytems linked to powerful computers provide realistic simulations of anything from Formula 1 racing to interstellar combat.

▷ A virtual reality station of 2015 will immerse the user's whole body in computer-generated sensations that completely replace the real world.

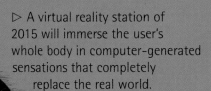

Face the fear

Virtual spiders have already been used to cure people who have an uncontrollable fear of real ones. Wearing virtual reality headsets, these people—called arachnophobes—can overcome their terror by being introduced to virtual spiders that gradually increase in size. In the 21st century, virtual reality will help people overcome many other fears and worries that prevent them from leading normal lives.

△ Norns, Grendels, and other virtual creatures are born, live, and die inside the computers that run the latest Artificial Life games. Scientists use similar software to learn how biological-based life forms evolve and interact.

◁ Virtual reality headsets will be standard equipment in homes of the 21st century. Their uses will range from entertainment to training and "conditioning"—helping the wearer overcome psychological difficulties and phobias, such as fear of spiders.

△ The first sound recording was made by the American inventor Thomas Edison in 1877. His phonograph originally stored sound on a cylinder covered with tinfoil.

ELECTRONIC ARTS

In 1997, an American orchestra gave the first-ever performance of Mozart's 42nd Symphony—even though Mozart only wrote 41 symphonies and had been dead for more than 200 years. The new symphony was the work of a computer, aided by a human composer who programmed the machine to write in the style of Mozart.

In the 21st century, more and more of the music we hear will be written and performed by computers. Paintings and sculptures created by computers may become commonplace, too. However, until computers have the capacity to feel and express emotions, it is doubtful whether computer art and music can ever match, let alone surpass, the best works created by humans.

△ Digital technology records and re-creates the work of composers and artists in high-definition sound and vision. In the 21st century, computers will be able to create original art and music.

▷ From vinyl records to digital tapes, recording quality has improved dramatically over the last fifty years.

Master discs

The first phonograph records could only play three minutes of music and had to be made one at a time. If one hundred copies were needed, the musician had to perform the same piece one hundred times! A century later, in the late 1990s, double-sided DVDs (Digital Versatile Discs) can store two hours of high-quality sound and video, and are produced in factories that stamp them out by the million.

△ Early phonographs used a needle to pick up vibrations from grooves in the record and fed them into the speaker horn.

△ One DVD can store as much data—sound or vision—as a million phonograph records from the 1920s.

Playback time

By 2010, instead of buying prerecorded discs, we will be able to download music (as well as movies) straight from the Internet. Memory cards no bigger than a postage stamp will store the music. These will be inserted into playback systems the size and thickness of a credit card. Today's personal stereos, CD, and DVD players will be seen only in museums, alongside old-fashioned phonographs.

△ In a modern recording studio, digital technology allows engineers to enhance recorded tracks in many different ways. Their creative input can be as important as that of the original performers.

◁ By 2015, 3–D holographic sculptures will be a centerpiece in many homes.

Noise pollution

As the world becomes a noisier place, an electronic sound system known as Active Noise Control will become an increasingly important feature of our lives. By creating sound waves that cancel out unwanted noise, Active Noise Control can create a pool of silence around you.

THE MOVING IMAGE

In the 1990s, one hundred years after the birth of the movies, computer-generated digital effects—from asteroids to talking pigs—have became commonplace. In the 21st century we can expect to see electronic movie stars replacing flesh-and-blood actors. When every frame of a film is a computer-processed image, new digital stars can be created, and old ones—such as Charlie Chaplin or Elvis Presley—can be brought back to life to feature in new productions. You may even get a chance to appear on the big screen yourself, in a personalized digital edition of your favorite movie.

△ The 1902 movie *A Trip to the Moon* was one of the first to use models and special effects. The French director George Méliès adapted tricks he had learned as a stage magician.

From film to chip

For 150 years after its invention in the 1839, photography was a chemical process. Still pictures were mostly recorded on film which had to be developed and printed in special laboratories. In the 1990s, digital cameras became commercially available. These do not require film. Instead they capture the image on a special microchip, ready to be viewed on a computer or television screen. For moving images, handheld camcorders first appeared in the 1980s, recording onto standard magnetic videotape, but by the late 1990s, digital movie cameras were beginning to replace these.

△ Special glasses allowed audiences in the 1950s to watch films in 3-D. Smell-O-Vision was another innovation of the period.

▽ Video technology provides one alternative to more traditional movie screens. This giant video wall in Poitiers, France, is made up of 850 high-definition screens.

△ In the 1880s, Eadweard Muybridge used a device called a Zoopraxiscope to project images of moving animals and people. The pictures were taken with 24 still cameras arranged in a row.

True to life

When color holographic video becomes available, we will at last be able to see films in ultrarealistic 3-D, instead of on a flat screen. Holography is a complex process that mixes light beams to re-create the true appearance of solid objects. Primitive holographic video has been demonstrated by Professor Stephen Benton at the Massachusetts Institute of Technology's Media Laboratory, but we will probably have to wait until after 2010 before the quality is good enough for general use.

△ Ordinary people will become movie stars, too, when digital techniques allow a person's image to be seamlessly integrated with the on-screen action. Holography will add the extra drama of three-dimensional imagery to these personalized movies.

TUNING IN

△ John Logie Baird successfully demonstrated television in the 1920s, using a large spinning disk to scan the image.

In the early days of television in the 1930s, there were reports of viewers dressing up in their best clothes. They believed that if they could see people on the screen, then the people on the screen could see them! By 2010, television really will be a two-way experience. An interactive television may not actually watch you all the time, but it will soon learn your viewing preferences and suggest programs of interest from the thousands of channels on offer. You will even be able to select your own camera angles for watching a football game, choose items to build up news reports, and give instant feedback on programs.

▷ The Freeplay radio is ideal for places with no electricity or where batteries are hard to obtain. A few turns of the winder powers the set for 25 minutes.

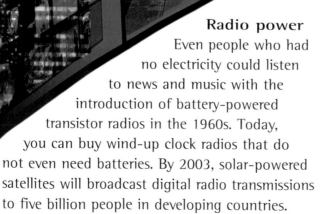

Radio power
Even people who had no electricity could listen to news and music with the introduction of battery-powered transistor radios in the 1960s. Today, you can buy wind-up clock radios that do not even need batteries. By 2003, solar-powered satellites will broadcast digital radio transmissions to five billion people in developing countries.

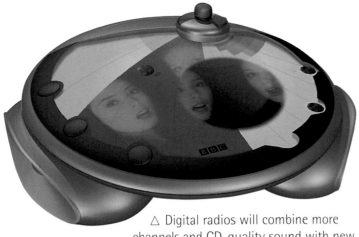

△ Digital radios will combine more channels and CD-quality sound with new facilities such as touch-screen displays and the ability to record programs.

Box of tricks

By 1998, some computers could receive television signals, and some digital televisions could be connected to the Internet. This marked the beginning of the merging of computers and television. By 2005, the telecomputer will be a feature of many homes. Television, radio, and a full Internet service will be available in a single unit.

▽ Hang-on-the-wall televisions first appeared in the late 1990s, when full-color, flatscreen plasma displays began to displace the much bulkier vacuum-tube screens used for the past 60 years.

▽ Floor-to-ceiling video screens may replace conventional walls and windows by 2020. A range of programs to suit the viewer will be selected automatically from the countless channels available.

Do-it-yourself

With the development of webcasting, anyone will be able to set up their own broadcasting station. Webstations are Internet sites that offer live sound and video, like broadcasting stations, where people can log on. By 2005, millions of webstations will be run by individuals or groups of people who share an interest.

Hamburger Abendblatt

Freitag, 19.30 MEZ — Tatort Dallas in Texas

Kennedy ermordet

Kopfschuß aus
dem Hinterhalt

Frau Kennedy
blieb unverletzt

Johnson neuer
US-Präsident

2025?

Medi-beds monitor health
and alert doctors

2020?

Four out of ten workers
based at home

1920s
Phone system links millions of homes to outside world

1971
Open University begins in Britain—students learn via TV

1997
Internet bookstores lead the way in online shopping

2003?
100 million computers are linked by the Internet

2007?
Online customized shopping for many items

2010?
People use Internet to vote in elections

2010?
Children around the world educated from home

2015?
Electronic communication centers in many homes

2015?
Most banking done on Internet

THE WORLD IN YOUR HOME

It took nearly a century for the number of telephones in the world to grow from one to a hundred million. By 2003, the number of computers on the Internet will have grown that much in just ten years, and the Internet will continue to expand faster than ever.

The Internet will link our homes to the outside world in all kinds of new ways, handling not only telephone and television, but a host of other activities including shopping, voting, and banking. Increasingly, people will learn and work from home, and even contact their doctor and be diagnosed via the Internet. Machines and domestic gadgets will be on the Net—cars, for example, will send e-mail to their owners when they need maintenance. By 2020, in the world's richer countries at least, the broadband Internet will be an essential part of life. Like the air we breathe, we will use it all the time without even thinking about it.

GLOBAL VILLAGE

When Admiral Nelson was killed in the Battle of Trafalgar in 1805, it took two weeks for the news to reach the papers in Britain. But when Diana, Princess of Wales, died after a late night car crash in Paris in 1997, a billion people around the world knew about it just a few hours later.

News travels fast in the modern world. In the 21st century, the nerve center of many homes will be the communications center. The communications center will not only receive the news, but will also be used for entertainment, education, or simply catching up with distant friends.

△ The Crimean War of the 1850s was the first in which the public was kept informed regularly of events. News reports were telegraphed back home and appeared in the papers the following day.

Shrinking world

Two hundred years ago, many people never ventured more than a few miles away from home. They had little contact with the outside world. In the 20th century, newspapers, radio, and television have given people a window on the world from their own homes. Since the mid-1990s, the Internet has been turning the world into a true "electronic village." Finding out what is happening thousands of miles away is just a matter of switching on your computer.

△ Radio news bulletins were a lifeline for families in Europe during World War II. Transmissions were often interrupted by fading sound and interference.

Personal service

By 2007, news will not be restricted to bulletins at fixed times. You will be able to specify what you want as well as when you want it—whether it is local or national news, or something of more personal interest such as the progress of a favorite team or stocks and shares. The computer will download specific items, compiling your own personal news bulletin.

▽▷ The communications center will be a major feature of future homes, with personalized news from near and far always available.

▷ When President John F. Kennedy was assassinated in November 1963, the news was broadcast to millions of people around the world.

▽ Images of our planet taken by satellites and spacecraft have underlined the fact that we are all part of a single global community.

Politics and power

By 2010, in many countries, presidents and governments will be elected by people voting from home on the Internet. Frequent referendums will give everyone a chance to vote on important decisions affecting their country or neighborhood. Some governments will use the Internet to inform people of how much tax to pay and transfer the money directly from their bank accounts.

ONLINE HOME

For most people, access to the Internet will mean a whole new range of services. Electronic shopping already exists, and many products, from books to airline tickets, can be bought over the Internet. With the introduction of electronic cash that can be used globally and personalized goods delivered directly from the manufacturer, conventional shopping will steadily decrease. It is estimated that by 2010, 20 percent of purchases will be made using the Internet.

Services other than shopping will also be available online. Possibilities include people in one country consulting medical experts in another country about their health, or farmers in remote areas downloading satellite pictures that provide information about their crops and livestock.

△ Supermarkets appeared in major cities during the 1950s and 1960s. Their main attraction was low prices and the novelty of selecting and handling goods yourself.

▽ △ A wide choice of on-line shopping is already available on the Internet. Choosing travel destinations, buying clothes, and ordering flowers are just a few of the many services.

Consumer choice

In the 21st century, customization—personalizing products according to buyers' specifications—will increasingly replace mass production. Using your computer, you will link up directly to the factories that make clothes, cars, and other products. A user-friendly interface will enable you to select colors, shapes, and other design features. If you want new clothes, lasers will scan your body to calculate the exact size. Finally, the finished product will be delivered directly to your door.

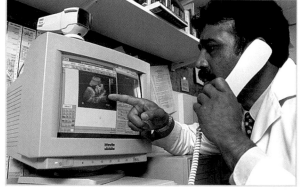

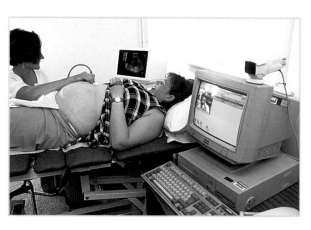

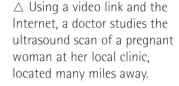

△ Using a video link and the Internet, a doctor studies the ultrasound scan of a pregnant woman at her local clinic, located many miles away.

▷ Cars will be one of many customized products available from automated factories. By feeding data directly from their home computers to the factory, customers will order a new model designed and built precisely to their own detailed specification.

The joys of shopping

Online shopping will increasingly replace visits to real stores. You will be able to create your own personalized shopping mall with instant access to all your favorite stores. Internet shopping will offer a wider variety of goods to choose from and at a much lower cost than real stores. For those who still think Internet shopping is hard work, intelligent agents will make shopping a stress-free experience. They will search out products that fit your requirements, automatically pay for them, and have them delivered to your door.

◁ A special shower unit with built-in sensors and a handheld "Mednet" scanner, planned for the year 2020, will monitor your health daily and communicate with online databases if they detect any problems.

Cashless society

Today, when people make a purchase over the Internet, they usually use their credit card. In the early years of the 21st century, electronic cash, or e-cash, will become commonplace, accepted worldwide for Internet purchases. Trials of e-cash based on smart cards have already proven successful. Eventually, there will be no need to carry real cash, and e-cash will also be used for the majority of non-Internet transactions.

LIVE AND LEARN

During the 1990s, the Internet has become a vast new information resource to help teachers and students. Virtual reality, with its ability to simulate the real world, will take the learning process one stage further. Pupils will make virtual visits to foreign lands to learn languages and study geography. Art students will explore virtual museums and galleries around the world, while drama students will be able to join fellow students in master classes with actors. Virtual reality will also provide highly effective interactive training for surgeons, pilots, military personnel, and many other people.

△ For centuries, textbooks have been an essential part of education. However, in the 21st century, new technologies will reduce their importance as learning tools.

△ Since the 1950s, children's television has done much to broaden the horizons and stretch the imagination of preschool children.

Online learning

By 2002, in some countries, every school, college, and library will be linked to a learning highway on the Internet. One of the many benefits is that students will be able to take correspondence courses in subjects not available at their own school. Students with their own connection to the highway will have the option of doing more of their work from home, while virtual schools will offer the same educational opportunities to those who live in very remote places.

▷ By 2005, when virtual reality has become available in the classroom and at home, students will have instant access to museums and galleries worldwide.

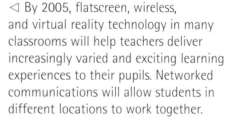

◁ By 2005, flatscreen, wireless, and virtual reality technology in many classrooms will help teachers deliver increasingly varied and exciting learning experiences to their pupils. Networked communications will allow students in different locations to work together.

World at your fingertips

Fifteen centuries ago, all the wisdom of the Western world was stored on half a million papyrus scrolls and housed in a single place—the libary at Alexandria in Egypt.

Today, people once again have access to vast amounts of knowledge in one place—their own homes—via the Internet and the information stored on DVDs and CD-ROMs.

Learning for life

Learning—driven by information technology—will be a lifelong activity, not just something you do when you are young. Rapidly evolving technology means that jobs will change much faster than in the past, so workers will need frequent retraining, assisted by virtual reality, to learn and build up new skills.

BLURRED VISION

Learning will become an effortless process according to this French postcard from 1910. It predicted that by the year 2000, knowledge will be transferred via electricity directly into the brain.

▷ It has been calculated that people who worked in cities during the 1990s spent the equivalent of three whole years of their lives battling through the rush hour on their way to and from work.

◁ Before the development of factories in Europe during the 1700s, whole families worked together at home making cloth and other products.

WORKING AT HOME

By 2020, four people in ten will be working from home instead of an office. Designers, architects, software engineers, and many others who use computers will no longer need to commute to work. These "telecommuters" will use the Internet and high-capacity optical links to keep in touch with their employers and clients, who may be in distant parts of the world. Telecommuting eliminates the need for the majority of a company's employees to assemble in a specific place each day. For those who miss the social aspects of the workplace, local centers will be set up where they can meet other workers.

△ In the 21st century, people such as architects will no longer gather in a single workplace. Instead they will be based at home, working together as a team linked by the Internet and other communication devices.

Teamwork

Whenever a new cathedral was built in the Middle Ages, craftsmen such as stonemasons and carpenters frequently traveled from distant parts of the country to work on the project. In the 21st century, a similar system will operate. To design a new aircraft, for example, highly skilled professionals, such as engineers and programmers, will form a team. But they will rarely meet one another. They will be linked instead by computer and will operate from their own workstations around the world.

Career prospects

In the 20th century, many people kept the same job for life. But by 2010, the idea of a long-term job will no longer be valid. Instead of taking a permanent job, many people will work on a succession of different projects. Computers and robots will continue to take over repetitive, manual jobs previously performed by humans—in banks and factories, for example. But new technologies will also create many new opportunities, such as in the entertainment and software industries.

△ Architects and engineers working in different countries pooled their resources to design one of the masterpieces of late 20th century architecture. The Guggenheim Museum in Bilbao, Spain, was built using advanced technology and high-tech materials such as titanium.

Job satisfaction

Telecommuting will result in increased productivity and improved morale as people will be able to spend more time with their families. Another related benefit will be a reduction in pollution caused by rush hour traffic. Telecommuting will not only transform our working practices, it will also affect where we live. We will no longer need to be based near or in big cities and future telecommuters will set up new communities wherever they wish.

2050
Flying micro robots used for surveillance

2015
Internet "immune system" protects it from all viruses

2010
Accurate weather forecasts available a month ahead

2005
Most Earth-threatening asteroids detected

1998
Over 20,000 computer viruses known

KEEPING WATCH

When Tony Bullimore, a British yachtsman, was trapped under the hull of his capsized boat in the Antarctic Ocean in 1997, his life was saved by space-age communications. An automatic beacon on his yacht sent out a radio signal that was picked up by a passing satellite and relayed to a control center in France. From there, an Australian ship was alerted to rescue him. In the 21st century, the microchip will help make life safer for many more people on the planet. In our homes, detectors and robot systems will warn us of dangers and automatically take action. Satellite positioning systems will mean that you need never get lost wherever you are in the world, and other satellites will give early warnings of hurricanes and earthquakes. Even the possibility of a devastating impact from space will be reduced by powerful hardware designed to detect and destroy asteroids.

1990s
Security cameras appear across many cities

1968
First clear photos of Earth taken from space

1930s
Weather ballons first sent to probe upper atmosphere

A.D. 132
In China, device invented for detecting earthquakes

HOMEWATCH

Today, millions of people depend on electronic intruder alarms and smoke detectors to feel safe in their homes. By 2020, many new homes will have intelligent security systems, connected by radio to a wide range of sensors hidden around the building. As well as detecting intruders and the first signs of smoke, a computerized system will monitor air and water pollution, and warn of harmful bacteria in the kitchen and other dangers around the house. The main system will be linked to a community system for extra security or to protect your home while you are away.

△ More than 2,000 years ago, the Romans used geese, which cackle loudly when disturbed, as an alarm system to warn them of an enemy invasion.

Unlocking doors

Keyless locks will be common in the 21st century, opening doors automatically when the right person approaches. Computers will use biometric technology to identify people. Some systems will scan and recognize a person by their voice or their face. Others will recognize fingerprints, the patterns on the iris of an eye, or even identify our DNA makeup—the genetic code that is unique to each one of us.

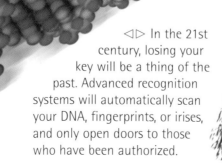

◁▷ In the 21st century, losing your key will be a thing of the past. Advanced recognition systems will automatically scan your DNA, fingerprints, or irises, and only open doors to those who have been authorized.

Ideal home

Smart homes will not only recognize us, but automatically respond to an individual's needs. Once a person has been identified—either by biometrics or a wearable microchip—the computer will operate a range of devices such as lights, heaters, air-conditioning, and even other computers. The intelligent building of 2020 will also be able to learn, remembering, for example, the user's preferences for lighting levels and room temperature.

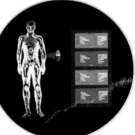

△ In 1998, Professor Kevin Warwick of Reading University in England had a small glass tube containing a microchip sewn into his arm. It allowed him to interact with his building, which opened doors for him and kept track of his movements.

Crime fighting

Microchips that allow devices to work only in the house they are purchased for will be one deterrent to burglars in the 21st century. If items are taken, they will send out a radio signal that can be tracked by the police. Internet crime and viruses may pose more of a challenge to security services. Criminal hackers and crime syndicates already use the Internet to gain access to secret information or illegally transfer money.

△ The Internet provides a breeding ground for computer viruses to wreak havoc on machines. An effective immune system that protects the Internet will be in operation by the second decade of the 21st century.

△ This robot guard is used in buildings to detect fire, steam, and gases. It uses video cameras and has temperature, smoke, and humidity sensors.

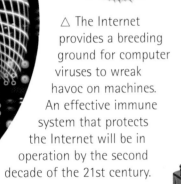

△ By 2005, affordable miniature video cameras will be widely available. People will be able to use these cable-free devices anywhere in the home.

CRYSTAL BALL

By 2050, insect-sized flying robots called bugbots could be in use, equipped with tiny cameras to send back pictures to a remote monitor. Fleets of bugbots will act as mobile security cameras. In the home, they could be used to watch over a baby.

◁ This ingenious earthquake detector was invented by a Chinese scientist nearly 2,000 years ago. Tremors dislodged a small ball from the central container into the mouth of one of the waiting frogs.

EARTHWATCH

Satellites have transformed the way we study our planet. In a few orbits, a satellite can provide a detailed survey of a remote or mountainous area that would take years to map from the ground. By 2005, more than 30 "Earthwatch" satellites will be studying the Earth from space. Some will check on weather systems and ocean currents, while others will measure air pollution, detect floods and forest fires, and keep watch for ships illegally discharging oil into the sea. It will also be possible to buy images of any point on the Earth's surface, showing details as small as three feet across or less.

Weather report

Before the launch of the first weather satellite in 1960, forecasts were based on just a few measurements from balloons and ground stations. By 2010, satellites and more computer power will make detailed 30-day forecasts possible. Effective ways of changing the weather will also be developed, such as treating clouds to prevent dangerous hailstorms from developing. By 2050, huge wind barriers could be in use to alter wind patterns and control the climate in various parts of the world.

△ Explorer II was one of the first balloons used by scientists to carry instruments into the upper atmosphere. In 1935, it reached an altitude of 13 miles and took the first photographs that clearly showed that the Earth's surface is curved.

◁△ A hurricane's distinctive swirling cloud pattern, 600 miles across, is easily spotted from space. For people on the ground, it can bring torrential rain and winds up to 155 mph.

Spaceship Earth

In the 1960s, the first photographs of the Earth taken from space dramatically changed the way we relate to our world. They made people realize that we live on a fragile, precious planet. With this came a new awareness about our responsibility to safeguard the environment. By 2020, it should be clear whether humans are winning the battle to preserve the Earth for future generations, or whether we are heading for a global catastrophe caused by pollution and the climate changes it produces.

▽▷ Bridges and buildings collapsed in the Kobe earthquake in Japan in 1995. A satellite image shows ground movements after a major earthquake.

Tremors

By 2025, according to some experts, it will be possible to predict exactly when earthquakes and other natural disasters are going to happen. It might even be possible to prevent some of the more devastating effects caused by them. Scientists, for example, may be able to stop earthquakes by pumping water into faultlines to prevent potentially catastrophic stresses from building up.

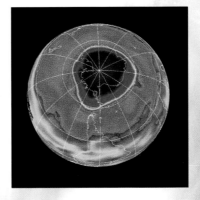

▷ The ozone hole over Antarctica stands out vividly in a false-color satellite image. The ozone layer, which protects the Earth from the Sun's ultraviolet rays, has been damaged by chemicals called chlorofluorocarbons (CFCs), which were once commonly found in aerosol spray cans.

◁ Meteosat Second Generation Craft are due for launch from the year 2000 onward. They will help scientists study violent storms and monitor changes in climate.

△ In 1908, a huge fireball flattened over 1,000 square miles near Tunguska, Siberia. Scientists believe it was caused when part of a comet exploded.

SPACEWATCH

▽ A new generation of optical telescopes is helping astronomers study how planets form around distant stars. The Very Large Telescope in Chile has a mirror 26 feet across.

In December 1997, a twelve-billion-year journey through space finally came to an end when light rays traveling from the most distant galaxy yet detected reached the world's largest telescope in Hawaii. It was one of many spectacular discoveries that astronomers have made by attaching supersensitive electronic eyes called CCDs (Charge-Coupled Devices) to their telescopes. In the years ahead, second-generation space telescopes and giant Earth-based instruments will reveal even more about the origin and structure of the universe. Closer to home, automated telescopes are already watching out for asteroids that threaten our safety on Earth. Another search, for signs of extraterrestrial life, will also be aided by increasingly powerful electronics.

▷ In 1965, Arno Penzias and Robert Wilson discovered radio waves left over from the Big Bang—the event that created the universe. They used a radio antenna that was orginally designed to pick up signals from the Telstar satellite.

Earth under threat

Scientists are concerned that there are thousands of near-Earth asteroids—space rocks hefty enough to cause catastrophic damage if they collide with the Earth. By 2005, computerized telescopes will have tracked down the most threatening ones, so that possible impacts can be predicted well in advance. But the main challenge is to develop ways of using rockets or lasers to break up asteroids far out in space, or nudge them into orbits that take them out of Earth's path.

▽ A plaque on the Voyager 1 spacecraft carries a message from the Earth describing who we are to any aliens who might intercept it.

△ As part of the search for extraterrestrial intelligence, the world's largest radio telescope, at Arecibo in Puerto Rico, sent out a coded signal in 1974.

Moon base

By 2050, a powerful transmitting station, built on the far side of the moon, could beam out messages by radio and high-powered laser to possible civilizations in distant parts of our galaxy. The station would run unmanned for many years, powered by its own nuclear reactor.

◁ Many science fiction movies have featured attacks by unfriendly aliens. In this 1953 poster for *War of the Worlds*, terrified humans flee Martian invaders.

The search for life

Many astronomers believe that the first step in detecting extraterrestrial intelligence is to locate planets orbiting distant stars. Imaging these planets is extremely difficult because they are small and dim, hidden in the glare of their local stars. There are proposals for arrays of space telescopes to be positioned near Jupiter, well away from dust in the inner solar system. These would be able to see planets directly as they orbit other stars. They might even be able to detect gases such as water vapor and ozone, suggesting a friendly climate and the existence of life.

△ High-energy lasers offer one possibility of preventing a catastrophic asteroid impact. Heat from the lasers vaporizes the asteroid's surface, causing it to give off jets of gas. These jets act like rockets, deflecting the asteroid away from Earth.

GLOSSARY

Analog A system or device that handles sound, pictures etc. directly as changing electrical vibrations, rather than by converting them into numbers (see digital).

Artificial Intelligence (AI) The ability of computers and robots to do some of the intelligent things that humans can do, such as thinking, reasoning, and interpreting pictures.

Broadband A communications system that can handle a large amount of information at high speed.

Byte A unit for measuring the amount of information stored or processed by a computer. There are about 100,000 bytes of text in this book.

Customization A system of manufacturing items such as cars or clothing in which each individual product is made to suit the requirements of a particular customer.

Digital A system or device in which sound, pictures, or other information is handled in the form of numbers. The alternative is an analog system.

Expert system Computer software that stores detailed information about a particular subject and uses it to answer questions.

Fiber optics Long, thin strands of glass through which digital information can be passed in the form of high-speed pulses of laser light.

Force feedback device Part of a virtual reality setup which makes users think that they are interacting with solid objects.

Holography A process that uses lasers to produce three-dimensional images.

Integrated circuit See **Microchip**.

Intelligent agent Software that acts as a personal assistant, helping its user find relevant information on the Internet. Sometimes known as a "knowbot."

Internet The worldwide network of millions of computers which can communicate with each other.

Knowbot See **Intelligent agent**.

Laser A device that produces a narrow, rapidly-varying beam of light or other radiation, used to carry information through fiber optics.

Microchip A small but complex electronic device in which millions of transistors and other components are mounted on a single slice of material, usually silicon, to form an "integrated circuit."

Microprocessor A type of microchip that can do calculations or control machinery. Microprocessors are the "brains" of computers and other devices.

Neural net A computer system in which electronic units link to each other in the same way that cells called neurons form a network in the human brain.

Packet switching The way information travels through the Internet, divided into "packets" of data that take different routes.

Quantum computer A proposed new type of computer that would use particles smaller than atoms to do millions of calculations at once.

Radio A way of communicating by sending electrical vibrations through space, without using wires or cables.

Sensor A device that provides a computer or microprocessor with environmental information such as temperature, sound, or light.

Simulation Using a computer to imitate the behavior of some other system, such as flying an aircraft or a dangerous situation in a nuclear power station.

Smart machine A machine or system that uses sensors and a microprocessor to make it behave in a clever way for example by anticipating or remembering the user's actions.

Telecommuter Someone who works at home rather than traveling to an office, using computers and communications technology to keep in touch with the outside world.

Telecomputer A combined computer and digital television set.

Transistor A tiny electrically-operated switch used in microchips.

Videophone A telephone whose users can see each other. Also known as a picturephone, or a holophone if it uses holography to produce three-dimensional images.

Virtual reality A system that creates an artificial environment in which everything that enters the user's senses is controlled by a computer, and the user's actions seem to make things happen in the environment.

Webcasting A system of broadcasting in which programs are played on websites and which listeners and viewers can access from their home computers via the Internet.

Website Text, graphics, and other effects produced by a person or organization, and stored in a computer accessible to other computers via the Internet.

World Wide Web The global network of interlinked websites.

WEBSITES

The following is a selection of websites related to all aspects of technology and the future.

The Philips' *Vision of the Future* site at **www.design.philips.com/vof/toc1/home.htm** is full of exciting ideas for future technology that will affect our lives in many ways.

For the latest news of developments in the world of computers, try the Computer Network CNET at **www.cnet.com**. Click on the "gadgets" link to find out about the latest communications technology.

To find out about some of the key inventions in the fields of communications and computers, visit the *Information Age* online exhibit at the National Museum of American History: **www.si.edu/resource/tours/comphist/computer.htm**

For information about robotics, try the NASA site at **robotics.jpl.nasa.gov**, which also includes links to other robot-related sites.

Android World at **www.android.com** is packed with information on android projects underway around the world, for both practical and entertainment purposes. It also includes a history of androids.

For a glimpse into the future of technology, visit *Science for the Millennium*, an online exhibition set up by the National Center for Supercomputing Applications at **www.ncsa.uiuc.edu/Cyberia/Expo**. It includes pages on computing, the role of technology in space exploration, and virtual reality.

Other sites devoted to the history of computers, communications technology, and other related topics can be reached using your favorite search engine.

PLACES OF INTEREST

Many museums and science centers around the country have displays and exhibitions that show the history of communications. Some of them also feature the latest and forthcoming developments. They include:

The National Museum of American History (Washington, DC) An exhibition entitled *Information Age: People, Information, and Technology* shows, visually and interactively, how information technology has changed our society over the last 150 years.

The Tech Museum of Innovation (San Jose, CA) Over 240 interactive, hands-on exhibits about the technologies that affect our daily lives. The *Communication Gallery* explores the ways in which technology is making this a smaller world by changing how we work, communicate, and share information.

The Computer Museum (Boston, MA) As well as exhibits on robots and networks, a comprehensive history of computers looks at the evolution, technology, and impact of computers.

The Museum of Science and Industry (Chicago, IL) The oldest science museum in the Western hemisphere and the first in North America to have hands-on, interactive exhibits that explore all aspects of science and how it affects our lives.

In the pipeline is **The San Francisco Computer Museum**, to be built in several stages over the next five years, with the goal of becoming a global center for the history and appreciation of technology.

INDEX

ACKNOWLEDGMENTS

The publishers would like to thank the following illustrators for
their contribution to this book:

Mike Buckley 34-35; Roger Harris 10-11, 26-27; Graham
Humphries 15br, 18br, 55br; Richard Holloway 27l, 38-39,
48-49, 58-59; Mark Preston 6-7, 8-9, 16-17, 18-19, 20-21,
22-23, 24-25, 30-31, 32-33, 36-37, 40-41, 42-43, 44-45,
46-47, 50-51, 52-53, 54-55.

The publishers would like to thank the following for supplying
photographs for this book:

Page 3 Slim Films; 6 tl Slim Films, cl BT Laboratories, c GJLP –
CNRI/SPL, bc Science Museum/Science & Society Picture Library;
6-7 c Tony Stone Worldwide/Ed Honowitz; 8 bl Science
Museum/Science & Society Picture Library, bc (abacus) Science
Museum/Science & Society Picture Library, bc Tony Stone
Worldwide/Ed Honowitz, tr GJLP-CNRI/SPL, cr BT Laboratories;
8-9 t Science Museum/Science & Society Picture Library,
b Science Museum/Science & Society Picture Library; 9 bl
Science Museum/Science & Society Picture Library, bc AT & T
Bell Labs/SPL, bcr Science Museum/Science & Society Picture
Library, br Psion; 10 tl Tony Craddock/SPL, cr AT & T Bell
Labs./SPL; 11 tl Popperfoto, tr Crown Copyright/Health & Safety
Laboratories/SPL; 12 tl George Bernard/SPL, cl Popperfoto, c Rex
Features/Nils Jorgensen, br Tony Stone Images/Mark Wagner;
13 t John Edward Linden/Arcaid, c BT Laboratories, cr The
Advertising Archive, br George Bernard/SPL; 14 tl AKG London;
14-15 b C.S. Langlois, Publiphoto Diffusion/SPL, (background)
Architects Design Partnership, London; 15 tl BT Laboratories, c
George Haling/SPL, cr Popperfoto; 16 cl Apple Macintosh, cr
Science Museum/Science & Society Picture Library, bc Hank
Morgan/SPL; 17 tl BT Laboratories, br Powerstock/Zefa; 18-19
cr The Bridgeman Art Library, London; 19 tl British Museum/E.T.
Archive; 20 bl The Advertising Archive, tc AKG/Bibliotheque
Nationale, tr Palazzo Ducale, Mantua/AKG/Eric Lessing; 20-21
GJLP-CNRI/SPL; 21 tl Tony Stone Images/D.E. Cox, cr Hank
Morgan/SPL; 22 tl Mary Evans Picture Library, tr NASA/Science
& Society Picture Library, bl Dennis O'Claire /Tony Stone Images,
bc Powerstock/Zefa, c Science Museum/Science & Society Picture
Library, cr British Museum/E.T. Archive, br Roger
Ressmeyer/Corbis; 23 bl Slim Films, c Science Museum/Science &
Society Picture Library; 24 tl Peter Newark's Pictures, cl Corbis,
bl Hulton Getty; 25 tl BT Archives, tc Science Museum/Science
& Society Picture Library, bl BT Laboratories; 26 tl Hulton Getty,
b UPI/Corbis-Bettmann, c Popperfoto, cr Tony Stone
Images/Doug Armand; 27 tc Jonathon Blair/Corbis; 28 bl Paul
Souders/Corbis, c Mary Evans Picture Library, br Mary Evans
Picture Library; 28-29 Slim Films; 29 br BT Laboratories; 30 cl
CERN photo, bl Corbis-Bettmann; 31 bc © Telehouse; 32 cl The
Ronald Grant Archive, bc Popperfoto, c Robert Opie Collection,
tc Christie's Images, tr The Ronald Grant Archive;
32-33 t Science Museum/Science & Society Picture Library;

33 cl Science Museum/Science & Society Picture Library, bl
Corbis/Everett, all other pictures – Robert Opie Collection;
34 tl Rex Features, cr Image Bank/Steve Bronstein; 35 cl Peter
Menzel/SPL, tr Electronic Arts, br Cyberlife, bc BT Laboratories;
36 tl SPL, bl John Howard/SPL, br Adrian Dennis/Rex Features;
37 tl C.S. Langlois, Publiphoto Diffusion/SPL; 38 tl Meliès/The
Ronald Grant Archive, bl The Ronald Grant Archive; 38-39 The
Ronald Grant Archive; 39 t The Bridgeman Art Library, London/
Stapleton Collection, tl IMAX; 40 tl Hulton Getty, cr Splash
Communications Ltd; 40-41 b BT Laboratories; 41 tl IDEO, tr
Philips Plasma; 42 tl BT Laboratories, tc Robert Opie Collection,
c Dr Jurgen Scriba/SPL, bc Hulton Getty; 42-43 t John Frost
Historical Newspaper Service, b Rex Features, tr BT Archives;
44 tl Hulton Getty, cr Popperfoto, bl BT Laboratories; 45 cr
Corbis/UPI, bc Popperfoto; 46 cl Hulton Getty/G.Craddock, cr
Rex Features/Nils Jorgensen, br Rex Features/Nils Jorgensen;
47 tl BT Laboratories, tr John Edward Linden/Arcaid, b BT
Laboratories; 48 tl Powerstock/Zefa, cl Ronald Grant Archive,
bl BT Laboratories; 49 tc Mary Evans Picture Library/Jean Marc
Cote, b Richard Bryant/Arcaid, br James King-Holmes/W
Industries/SPL; 50 tr Tony Stone Images/Stewart Cohen, cl Mary
Evans Picture Library, tr Rex Features/Patrick Barth, bl Tony
Stone Images/Jon Riley; 50-51 Softroom/J. Jones and T. Spencer;
51 tr Tony Stone Images, cr Rex Features/Patrick Barth, br Tony
Stone Images; 52 c (Meteosat Satellite) European Space Agency;
53 cl Jerry Mason/SPL, c Science Museum/Science & Society
Picture Library; 54 tl Mary Evans Picture Library; 55 bl Philips, c
Cybermotion, Inc.1998, cr INS/Brian Hatton; 56 b Tony Stone
Images/Ernest Braun, tc Science Museum/Science & Society
Picture Library; 57 bl European Space Agency, c Nasa/SPL, tr
Popperfoto/Reuter; 58 tl SPL/Novosti Press Agency, bl SPL/David
Parker, br SPL/AT & T Bell Labs; 59 cl The Ronald Grant
Archive/ Paramount Pictures, t Planet Earth Pictures, tr
NASA/SPL.

Key: b = bottom, c = center, l =left, r = right, t = top

Every effort has been made to trace the copyright holders
of the photographs. The publishers apologize for any
inconvenience caused.

Special thanks to Ian Pearson and Andy Gower
at BT Laboratories.